DOGA

Yoga for you and your Dog

Lisa Recchione
Foreword by Nora Hawkins

LISA RECCHIONE YOGA
Wellness, Growth, Joy

ISBN: 0615976174
ISBN-13: 978-0615976174

DEDICATION

This book is dedicated to all dogs, who I believe are the embodiment of love and light. I also dedicate this book to the SPCA of Tampa Bay, which provides shelter, care, and love for animals and their people.

CONTENTS

FOREWORD

My dog and I went to our first doga (rhymes with "yoga") class in January 2012. I had enthusiastically recruited Lisa Recchione to teach the class on behalf of SPCA Tampa Bay where I work. My thought, and that of our CEO, Martha Boden, was that a doga class would add a new twist to the many classes we offer through the SPCA's Sniff University program.

Along with eleven other dogs and their humans, my dog and I participated in a relaxing hour of massage, stretching and meditation.

The dogs may have gotten the best of it. At one point they got to lie on their backs while we humans massaged their tummies and stretched over them. Every one of our dogs grinned in doggie nirvana.

Some poses are easier with small dogs. Some are better with larger dogs. The St. Bernard owner in our class found it a bit tough to stay in pose while her dog rolled over on his back to bat his paws at her and give a few playful wet kisses. I did just fine with my ten-pound Dachshund, who stared up at me, rolled her eyes and gave me that *what the heck are you doing?* look.

I thoroughly enjoyed the hour. I left happy and peaceful. My dog slept all the way home. SPCA Tampa Bay has been welcoming students to doga for two years now.

Lisa and I hope you will enjoy learning how this wonderful partner yoga practice can help you and your dog relax and bond.

Nora Hawkins, MBA
Managing Director/Guest Services & Promotions
SPCA Tampa Bay

P.S. Check out our doga classes and free pet behavior helpline at www.SPCATampaBay.org.

INTRODUCTION

What the heck is doga?

I get that question all the time. Doga is a type of partner yoga people can do with their dogs. The reaction to that answer ranges from 'oh, how cool' to 'you have to be kidding me.' When first asked to teach doga, my reaction was both skeptical and cautious.

I had been teaching yoga and meditation for many years and I was also a dog parent. So when Nora from the SPCA of Tampa Bay asked me to teach a yoga class for dogs and their owners, I did some research and found very little on the topic. I ordered one of the few books I could find and watched a DVD. Then I started incorporating yoga poses as I worked with my dogs.

As we bent and posed, their expressions were hilarious. Prior to this my dogs would watch me or lay nearby while I practiced yoga. Now I was actively involving them in the practice! I quickly realized that this shared activity offered us enjoyable one-on-one time to bond and relax. I adapted yoga postures and breathing exercises to include my dear ones. During this time my mind was focused solely on them. I found the experience enjoyable and uplifting. The more I relaxed, the more they relaxed.

When we started teaching the very first SPCA doga classes in January 2012, my students experienced the same feelings of peacefulness and relaxation. I am now convinced that doga is an effective form of yoga, offering many of the same benefits to our canine companions as it offers to us. Plus, the practice strengthens the beautiful bond shared between us and our dogs.

Is Doga Yoga?

Yoga is often defined as the union of mind, body and spirit. The word *yoga* is a Sanskrit word meaning *to yoke or merge*. Yoga was the original holistic practice of integrating mind, body and spirit or higher awareness. These three things are not exclusive. The body and mind are interrelated and both affect and are affected by awareness. Yoga practitioners believe that if the body is healthy, the mind is tamed and some level of self-actualization is attained, allowing one to live a happy, fulfilling, and bountiful life.

The physical practice of yoga is intended to keep the body healthy and includes: postures (asanas), physical exercises, breathing practices, mental focus and awareness, energy work, diet, and lifestyle suggestions.

The mental practice of yoga includes techniques to help us understand and manage our minds: awareness of how our mind works, mental focus, thought focus, meditation, staying present and being mindful. Breathing techniques, physical practice, and energy work all calm the mind.

The spiritual aspect of yoga helps us to connect to our higher selves and a higher consciousness. Yoga is not a religion nor is it linked with any organized religion. The roots of yoga came from the ancient Indian texts called the Vedas, but yoga is not synonymous with Hinduism. The ideas of yoga have been applied to many faiths. Yoga is a way to connect to your highest self. Some people see this as the soul, infinite self, true self or higher mind.

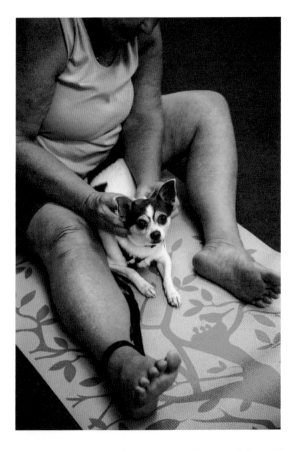

If you are spiritual you can relate to this as the part of you that always was, is, and will be. If you are not spiritual consider it a part of your consciousness that is aware of all other parts, the witness, and the super-conscious. This higher self is the part of us that elevates and moves us toward love, compassion, and connection. Tapping into this part of ourselves allows us to see meaning through intuition and insight. It is though this part that we feel connected to a higher consciousness. For the spiritual person this may be God, the universe, or energy. For the non-spiritual person this can be related to a peak experience, like seeing a beautiful panorama and feeling inspired and uplifted. This experience is often non-verbal; it rises from within and fills us with a sense of optimism, joy, and meaning.

The Beauty of Yoga

Yoga is versatile; we can take from it what we need or want. You can choose from many different styles ranging from primarily physical practices to deeply spiritual ones. The outcome is that we usually finish feeling better.

Many research studies have detailed the benefits of yoga. The regular practice of yoga benefits every system in the body: muscular, skeletal, cardiovascular, pulmonary, nervous, digestive, lymphatic, endocrine, integumentary, immune, respiratory, and reproductive. Today, yoga is used therapeutically to manage stress and stress-related illnesses. It is used to improve back health and to help people with specific conditions like Arthritis, MS, Fibromyalgia, Parkinson's, Alzheimer's, Depression, Insomnia, and more.

What makes yoga different from other exercise?

The combination of physical action, breathing practices, and mental focus makes yoga unique and particularly beneficial. So how does it benefit you and your dog?

Doga is a form of partner yoga: yogic practices done in pairs or even groups. In doga the physical postures and breathing exercises are done with our dogs. We always maintain contact with our pet in some way. Our mental focus is on our canine friend and our minds are completely in the present moment. Our awareness is elevated through the feelings of the deep love and connection we share with our dogs. For most of us, it is impossible to look at our pets without feeling like our hearts are going to explode with joy.

How do we benefit?

Doga gives us all the benefits of yoga. We relax through breathing techniques, stretching and posture, meditation and guided relaxation. When we are relaxed, our dogs relax too. They feed off our emotions. Our dogs are like our own little biofeedback machines. They know when we are calm or exited.

How do our dogs benefit?

In doga, our canine friends are able to spend completely uninterrupted time with us. They become our sole focus. They relax through our stroking, massage, and manipulation. Sensing that we are relaxed, our dogs are able to relax. Doga can be the perfect introduction to socialization for shy and timid dogs. Because doga is done in a group setting, it helps our canines build their confidence.

1 BASIC GUIDELINES

Before we begin, it's helpful to familiarize ourselves with some basic guidelines for humans and their canine pals.

First, let your dog be a dog. Let go of all expectations about how your dog should behave. You are doing this to strengthen your bond with your dog through an enjoyable shared activity. Never force your dog into a position or force her/him to sit quietly. Dogs are going to bark, walk around, sniff and be distracted. Let them, and then gently bring them back to the activity. I find that even if dogs are hesitant at the beginning they usually settle in and love the experience as the practice advances. Sometimes we have twenty dogs in class and they are lively at first, but by the end of class everyone is mellow and relaxed. Just imagine! Twenty dogs and their people all lying down for relaxation. When you practice at home the distractions are still present: someone comes to the door, the phone rings, something makes a noise only your dog can hear, etc. Let your dog react and then bring him back to the mat.

Next, be safe. Never force yourself into a stretch or position that causes pain. You are doing this to better your health, not cause injury. If you need to, modify the postures with chairs, blocks, blankets, or pillows. Only do something if it feels right and pay attention to your sensation in a pose.

When practicing with a dog you may find the normal form and action of postures to be a challenge. Yoga postures are designed with consideration of alignment, anatomy and balance. In a regular yoga class we pay attention to this and modify to avoid injury. In a doga class it is sometimes difficult to adhere to the classic alignment of poses because we are incorporating our dogs. This is why we must be very aware of how our bodies are feeling and adapt in a safe way.

Also, be present, aware, and *connect with love*. Set aside special times to practice with your dog and try to minimize distractions. Make your dog the focus of this activity. When we do other things with our dogs we often are only half-present. They lie near us when we watch TV. We talk on the phone or let our minds wander when we walk them. So make your doga time a special activity where you can truly observe and connect. It is good mental training for you and your dog will love it. This is an opportunity to focus on the deep, unconditional love we share with our dearest companions.

Basic precautions for us humans include:

- Keeping your spine neutral – never overarch any of the natural curves in your back. You have four natural curves in your spine: the cervical (neck), thoracic (ribs), lumbar (lower back), and sacral (base of spine). Never over stretch or strain.

- Protect your lower back. You want to support your lower back with your core muscles. Draw in and up on the mid- lower abdomen as you pull up on the pelvic floor and draw the sacrum in and up. In other words, draw in and up on the anus and sex organ as you pull in on your navel center (the mid-lower abdomen). This practice is called Mula Bhanda. It helps bring your pelvis into a neutral position and protects the lower back.

- Avoid over-rounding your upper back in a forward position. Draw in and up on your navel center and lift to the center of your breastbone. Draw your shoulder blades together toward your spine so you are stretching your chest from shoulder to shoulder in front.

- Keep your neck long in back and never over-flex the neck in any direction.

- To release a muscle group, tighten the corresponding opposite group. This is called reciprocal inhibition. For example when you tighten the quadriceps (front thigh) it will help the hamstrings (back thigh) release.

- When standing, establish your balance and keep the muscles of your feet and legs active.

- When folding forward, hinge at the hips and use your core muscles to protect your spine.

- When twisting, start from the base of your spine and move up, using your core muscles to protect your spine.

Basic precautions for our dogs include:

- Never force your pet into a pose.

- Watch their reactions, especially when you are stretching their spines, twisting, or moving their joints.

- Watch for hot spots, lumps, or any signs of discomfort during massage. If you find or feel something that puzzles you, consult your veterinarian at your earliest convenience.

- Finally, have fun! I have had some of my greatest laughs in doga sessions. Go into it with an open mind and heart.

2 GENTLE PRACTICES TO HELP YOU BEGIN

The following poses are accomplished while in an easy sitting pose or in a chair. If sitting cross-legged is difficult for you, try sitting on folded blankets, a rolled mat, firm pillows, or a block.

Keep at least one hand or a part of your body touching your dog. Sometimes it's easier to move yourself around your dog. For some positions our dogs will be in front of us or at our sides. A small dog can rest in your lap. Larger dogs can sit close to you. The connection with your dog is meant to be physical, mental, and emotional. Be sure to focus on your dog. Make eye contact. Caressing, kissing and loving is always appropriate.

Shoulder Shrugs

Lift your shoulders up toward your ears and inhale. Lower your shoulders down and exhale. This is a great exercise to relieve stress in our upper trapezius muscles. You can also inhale through a rounded open mouth and exhale through a wide, open mouth. This will relieve tension in your jaws.

Neck, Side to Side

Inhale and turn your head left. Exhale and turn your head right. This releases tightness in the neck.

Ear to Shoulder

Bring your right ear to your right shoulder and take five deep breaths. Then, bring your left ear to your left shoulder and take five deep breaths. This stretches one of the tightest muscles in our necks.

Spinal Flex

Arch your spine forward as you inhale and arch back as you exhale. You are lifting up the chest bone as you flex forward and pulling the belly in as you exhale. Try to focus on the spine only. Don't move your neck or head. This increases flexibility in the spine, keeps the disks subtle, and actually moves cerebral spinal fluid. It is also good for your brain.

Hip Rolls

Keep knees wide and rotate the torso from the hips in a circle. Keep the spine in alignment as you rotate. Press your hands into the knees to gain leverage. This exercise is a great way to open the hip joints.

Seated Twist

Position your dog to the right of you. Place your left hand on your pet. Take your right hand and place it behind you. Inhale and align the spine by drawing in on your navel and your pelvic floor, bringing the tailbone in to neutral. Lift the chest while keeping shoulders down. Use your abdominal muscles to twist.

Begin to twist to the right starting from the bottom of the spine. Turn lower ribs right, mid ribs right and top ribs right. Turn your head last. Take five breaths. Repeat to the left.

Twists are great for the spine and strengthen the core. They are said to be cleansing because they squeeze the digestive system.

You can also twist holding your dog at your chest, if your dog is small enough. Remember to twist with your core. You can twist side-to-side in a slow movement, inhaling as you twist one way and exhaling as you twist the other way, or hold the twist.

For large dogs, pull your pet up and twist with him in your arms.

Cow-Faced Pose

In a seated position lift your right arm up and turn your palm toward your head and then facing back. Bend your right elbow and bring your fingers to your upper back between the shoulder blades. Take your left arm out parallel to the floor. Take the back of the left hand to your back and turn your palm to face back with the thumb up. Bend your elbow and bring the back of your hand to your lower shoulder blades. Now try to inch your hands toward each other trying to make contact. Squeeze your lower ribs into the spine and keep your shoulders down.

Eagle Pose

Bring your hands in front with the palms facing each other. Cross your left elbow over your right and bend the elbows bringing your forearms parallel with your chest. Keep your shoulders down as you lift your elbows slightly, pressing your forearms together. This is a nice stretch for the upper back. If your hands don't touch you can just bring your forearms together as much as possible or grip a strap between your hands.

Rock Pose

Come into a kneeling position where you are sitting on your heels. You can sit on a block or two blocks to protect your knees. This stretches the quadriceps. The name comes from an old saying: if you eat in this pose, it will help you digest rocks.

Not that I'd recommend that you do, of course.

3 STRETCHING AND FLEXING
FOR YOUR DOG

We will now do some manipulation for our dogs. Please be aware of your dog's reaction and never force a pose.

Dog Spine Extension and Twist

From a kneeling, sitting or ting position behind your dog, interlace fingers on your dog's ribs and pull your dog upward to be supported by your body. Twist your dog to the left and then to the right. Then position your hands around your dog's hips and gently stretch up. Gently lift the hind legs.

Joint Flex for Dogs

Begin by moving your dog's front leg forward and back. Then flex the paw, then just the knee and then move the shoulder. Do this to all four limbs separately. Stay focused on your dog and be aware of any signs of pain or discomfort. This exercise may be painful for older or arthritic dogs. In this case, simply massage the painful joint. Once the joints are lubricated you can extend the dog's front leg, then the opposite back leg and repeat. Slowly do one leg at a time.

All-Fours Pose for You and Your Dog

Start with your hands in line with your elbows and your shoulders. Have your knees under your hips. Your dog can be under you or in front of you. You can use a blanket or double mat under your knees for cushioning.

Cat Cow

This is a deep spinal flex for you. Arch your spine down toward the floor. Your belly will drop down and your head gently lift to look up. You start by lifting the

tailbone up while you slowly drop your belly and spine, then gently lift your head. Your dog can be under you or in front of you. Having your dog in front allows you to kiss her/him when your head is low!

Then do the opposite. Tuck your tailbone down and then raise the spine towards the ceiling. Draw the belly upward. Bring your chin down toward your chest. You should feel a stretch in your spine and between your shoulder blades. Inhale as your belly drops and exhale as you lift your spine. This is a great warm up for your spine and core.

Thread the Needle

From all-fours, take one arm under the torso and lead it toward the opposite shoulder taking the hand past the opposite shoulder and past the body frame. The extended arm is straight and rests on the floor. Then extend your spine back and press the shoulder of the extended arm into the floor to get a good stretch on the shoulder pressing into the floor. You can touch your dog with the extended hand or place your dog under you.

Leg Extensions for You

From all-fours extend one arm straight in front and the opposite leg straight in back. Support your spine by drawing your navel in. Stretch through your extended fingers and extended toes. You can do this facing your dog or over your dog.

Child's Pose and Wide-Leg Child's Pose with Your Hands on Your Dog

From all-fours, reach your arms forward and place your hand on your dog. Then fold back bending your knees and resting your torso on your thighs. Extend from the base of your spine to your fingertips. You can do this with your hands on your dog or over your dog.

Puppy Pose

From all-fours stretch your arms forward as you would in child's pose. Lift your hips high off the ground and stretch back. This stretches the spine. You can do this with your hands on your dog or over your dog.

Down Dog

From all-fours, make sure that the line of your wrists line up with the front of the mat. Spread your fingers. Make sure your hips are in line with your knees or have your knees a little further back. Turn your inner elbows to face up toward the ceiling. Reach your hips back and start to extend the spine. Start with your knees bent. Draw your navel in and lift your hips and bottom toward the ceiling. Start with your legs bent and then gradually straighten if you can. Draw your shoulder blades down your back and rotate your upper outer arms down. Draw your navel in and up and keep your tailbone down in neutral. Draw the front of your thighs back as you stretch the hamstrings and calves. Press down through your heels. Your heels may not touch the floor. Theoretically you should have a pretty straight line from your forearms to your hips.

You can do this facing your dog or over your dog. Our dogs bow to us in this pose every day. Now it is our turn to honor them.

4 STANDING POSES

The following poses are done in a standing position. Sometimes standing up can make our dogs more active. You may have to hold or pet your dog after you stand to calm him again.

Mountain Pose, Standing in Alignment

Stand with your feet hip-distance apart. Lift and spread your toes and then lower them. Line up your ankles, hips, and shoulders. Make sure your weight is evenly distributed on both sides of your feet and also on your heels and your big toe and little toe mounds. Press your big toe mound down while turning your shin out. This should lift the arches of your feet. Lift from the front ankle to the hip. Draw the top thighs back. Lift from the back of the knee to the buttocks. Draw your navel in and up as you draw your tailbone in. Make sure your hips are balanced--not too far forward or too far back. Draw the tips of your shoulder blades together in back to stretch and open your chest. As you lift your sternum, draw your shoulders down. Turn your palms facing forward. Reach down as you lower your shoulders and lift your chest. Slightly tuck your chin and extend the back of your neck.

Feel the alignment as you stand and take a few breaths. If you have a small dog, you can pick the dog up and hold your dog at your chest. If you have a big dog, stand by your dog and make contact with your leg.

Half Forward Fold

Stand in front of your dog. Your dog should be sitting facing you. From this standing pose take your hands to your hip creases and fold down (bend) from there. Keep your navel drawn in and fold until your hands reach your dog's shoulders. Keep your spine extended. Tighten the front of your legs and fold forward, hinging from the hips. Press the tops of your thighs back and keep your tail tucked in. You only fold half way at first and then slowly fold lower each time you come down.

You can move from the half fold to the full fold. From the half fold, inhale and extend the spine. Then lower to the full fold and stroke your hands down your dog's back. Inhale and extend up and exhale and lower down. You are stroking your dog each time you fold down.

Full Forward Fold Pose with Hands on Your Dog

This is the same posture as the Full Forward Fold but you stay in the forward fold and stroke your dog.

Wide-Leg Forward Fold

Your legs should be three to four feet apart. Start with your feet parallel and then point your toes inward, pigeon-toe style. Your dog should be in front of you and between your legs. You fold down from the hips, keeping the navel in and up, tailbone in and neutral, and chest lifted. Place your hands on the dog. This is similar to what we did in the first forward fold. You start out folding half way. With your hands on your dog's shoulders inhale and extend the spine and then exhale and lower to a deeper fold. It's fun to kiss your dog's head as you stroke down the back.

Twist, Please

From here you can take a twist by placing one hand on your dog and twisting the torso upwards as you lift your other hand. Use your core to support the twist.

Warrior 2 Pose

From standing pose step your feet out about three to four feet apart. Start with your feet parallel. Turn your the toes on your back foot in about a quarter of the way. Turn your front leg out at a ninety degree angle so that your toes point to the front of the mat. Make sure that the heel of your front foot lines up with the inner arch of your back foot.

Bend your right knee to a right angle or slightly less than a right angle. Keep your hips level by lifting your front hip and lowering your back hip. Draw your navel in and up as you bring your tailbone into neutral.

Take your arms out to your sides and stretch them out from your body, parallel to the floor. Lift your chest bone and draw your shoulder blades together in he back. Stretch from fingertip to fingertip. Keep the back of your neck long with chin slightly drawn in and look towards your front hand. This is the traditional warrior 2 pose.

Now we will modify it for your dog partner. If you have a large dog you will line up your front leg so that it touches your dog. If you have a medium or small dog, you could step over your dog so that your dog is between your legs. If you have a very small dog you could hold your dog in your arms. Remember to keep your chest lifted. If yours is a very, very small dog, hold it with your back arm and extend your front arm.

Side Stretch Pose

Your feet and legs should be in the same position as Warrior 2. Place your dog on the inside of your bent knee. Then lower your torso toward the bent knee and either bring your elbow to the bent knee or brace a straight arm against the inside of the leg. It is with this hand that you try to touch your dog. If you can't reach your dog just rest your front leg against the dog.

Watch that your bent knee does not turn in. Your top hand stretches up. Turn your palm to face forward and then lift that arm so that it reaches over your head. Turn your outer upper arm toward your chest and your chest toward the arm. Keep your navel in and up. Your tailbone should be drawn in to neutral.

Warrior 1 Pose

This is a squared hip pose. Step back with one leg and place your back foot at a forty-five degree angle. Then bend your front knee to as close to a right angle as you can manage. Draw the front hip back and the back hip forward to square your hips. Turn your outer back calf out and your inner back thigh in and press down through the outside of the back foot.

Keep your weight evenly distributed on both feet. Bring your navel in and up and your tailbone in to neutral. Lift from your navel to your breastbone and chest. You can hold a small dog in your arms and work the bottom part of the pose. If you want to complete the pose or have a larger dog, place the dog by your front bent leg and make contact between your leg and your dog. Then reach your arms straight overhead. Keep your elbows straight and your palms facing each other. Draw your shoulder blades together and turn your outer upper arms forward, inner arms back. Keep your neck long and gently look up.

Triangle Pose

Your legs should be in the same position as Warrior 2. Make sure that the heel of your front foot lines up with the inner arch of your back foot. You will want to keep both legs straight. Your back leg then rotates in so that the kneecap faces front. Press into the outside of the back foot and lift the inner thigh of back leg. Spiral your front hip out by pressing your big toe and front inner heel into the floor. Bend your torso sideways toward your front leg and bring your hand to your dog. Your dog should be sitting or standing at the outside of your front calf.

With a big dog this is not hard. With a little dog it may be too far to stretch. You can place your small dog on a chair so that your reach is not too far. You can also position the dog by your front leg and make contact with your leg. You can then reach straight up with your top arm turning your top ribs back to open the chest. Keep your navel in and your tailbone in neutral. You can caress your dog with your lower hand.

Tree Pose

From a standing pose, shift your weight to one leg and center your balance evenly on that foot. Bend your other leg and externally rotate your hip so that your knee faces to the side. Place your foot on the calf or thigh of the leg you are standing on. *You do not want to place your foot on the knee of your standing leg.* If you have a small dog you can hold your dog in your arms or even lift your dog overhead. If you have a larger dog you would position the bent knee where it touches your dog.

Squat Pose

Place your feet mat-width apart with your heels on the mat and your toes pointing out at a forty-five degree angle. Your toes should be off the mat. Bend your knees and lower yourself into a squat. Your hands should be on your dog.

Lunge Pose

This is a squared hip pose, meaning that your hips stay level with each other as viewed from the front.

Start with your dog on the outside of your front knee and step back with one leg into a lunging position. You can leave your knee off the ground or place it on the floor. The hand by the front bent knee rests on and caresses your dog. Reach up with your other hand. Be careful that your front knee does not go over your ankle. Draw the navel in and up and bring your tailbone in to neutral. Lift from your navel to your breastbone. Draw your shoulder blades together and lift your chest.

5 MORE FLOOR WORK

Staff Pose

In a seated position, place your dog in your lap or across your thighs. For larger dogs, sit them by your side. Extend your legs out in front and sit with your hips at a right angle. Flex your ankles and draw your toes towards you. Tighten the front of your legs and pull up toward the torso. Draw your navel in and up and bring your tailbone in to neutral. Draw from the navel to the center of the breastbone. Roll your shoulders back and draw your shoulder blades together to lift the chest. Have your hands at your side and keep your elbows straight. Press your hands into the ground with your fingers together pointing forward. Extend your spine by grounding through your seat and legs and lifting up the spine to the top of the head.

Boat Pose

Start with your legs extended straight in front as you did in the Staff Pose. Bend your knees and place your feet flat on the floor. Have your dog in your lap or by your side. Then lean back on the soft part of your buttocks (do not put pressure on your tail bone) and balance. Tighten your abdomen and extend your spine. Draw your navel in and lift to the center of your chest. Keep your core strong. Balance and try to lift one foot off the floor. Try to lift the other foot. Your calves should be parallel to the floor. Then try to lift both calves at the same time.

You can pet your dog either in your lap or on the floor by your side. Work on straightening both legs; in time you should be able to do it.

Bridge Pose

If you have a smaller dog you would do this above the dog. Large dogs can remain at your side while you keep in contact with them.

Start seated with your legs extended in front of you and bend your knees over your dog. Move your buttocks as close to your dog as you can. Keep your feet in line with your hips and parallel to each other. Turn your shoulder blades toward each other on the floor. Keep your arms by your sides. Your palms should be face down.

Lift your hips and tighten your hamstrings and buttocks. Draw your navel in and up and lift your chest. Press your arms into the floor.

A more advanced version can be done with a smaller dog. Just place your dog on your lower abdomen and lift your dog up.

Table Pose

You can do this over any size dog. Come in to this position the same way you came into bridge pose. Start with your legs bent over your dog. Place your hands behind your hips with fingers facing either forward or back, whichever feels most comfortable. Lift your hips and torso while keeping your knees and shoulders in a straight line. Your abdomen and back muscles will work together to keep you lifted. Engage your buttocks and thighs. Your head can look forward or drop back, but be careful of your neck if you allow it to drop back. Do not overextend your neck.

Advanced yoga students who regularly practice backbends can do a full backbend pose. Your dog can remain under you or sit on your belly.

Cat Stretch Pose

Lie on your back with your dog by your side next to your upper right thigh. Draw your left knee to your chest and hold the pose for a few breaths. Than take your knee across in a twist to the left. Let your knee rest on your dog. Your arms should be perpendicular to your body. Try to keep your left shoulder on the ground. Repeat on the other side.

Seated Stretches

Note: If seated stretches are uncomfortable for you, elevate yourself from the floor by sitting on one or two folded blankets.

Bound Angle Pose

This is similar to a simple seated pose. Balance on your sit bones (the pelvic bones you sit on). Draw your navel in and up and bring your tailbone to neutral. Lift from your navel to the center of your breastbone. Draw your shoulder blades together to open your chest. Keep your shoulders down and your neck long.

Bring the soles of your feet together and extend your knees out to the side. Have your small dog either in front of your feet or between your legs. Caress your dog as you inhale. As you exhale, fold over to a slight forward angle.

Seated Leg Stretch

Take your legs out to the sides, keeping your knees straight. Bend your right knee and bring the sole of your right foot to rest on the inside of your left thigh, close to your groin. Have your dog between your legs, resting on the inside thigh of your extended left leg.

Take your left hand to your dog, leaning to the left until you feel a stretch on the right side of your body. Take your right hand out straight and then bend your elbow and place the back of your right hand on your back. Reach back with your right shoulder until you feel a slight twist to the right. Look over your right shoulder.

You can also reach your right arm over to the left. Lift your arm up and turn your palm to face left, and then stretch over to the left. Repeat to the other side.

6 MASSAGE

Massaging your dog is a wonderful bonding experience. Your focus is completely on your partner. Massage has been reported to have numerous health benefits for your dog including pain reduction, increased immunity, and stress reduction. Stress can make any condition worse.

Stress reduction through massage is one of the best gifts

we can give our dogs. Regular massage can also serve as a diagnostic tool to assess your dog's skin and observe reactions to any sensitive areas.

We can use two types of massage with our dogs. The first is a light effleurage using our fingertips and longer strokes. The second is a deep tissue massage using three fingers to isolate and relieve tight muscles.

Effleurage

This light massage begins with long strokes from the top of your dog's head to the base of your dog's rump. This long steady stroke, accomplished with a light touch, is very relaxing for your dog. Stroke the back of his head, jaw, neck, shoulders, front legs, paws, chest, belly, back to rump, hips, hind legs, paws, and tail.

Let your fingers search hot spots and be sensitive to your dog's reaction if you touch a particular area. This is an opportunity to notice lumps, sore joints, painful spots, etc. Doing this regularly will let you develop a baseline of your dog's skin and you'll know how his surface muscles usually feel.

Deep Tissue Massage

This type massage is performed with the index, middle and ring fingers. Now you press a little harder and isolate muscles to relieve tension and tightness. Again, be very aware of your dog's reaction to your touch. Don't press too hard or you may cause pain.

Massage in this order: back of neck to rump, head and neck including jaw shoulder and front legs, chest and abs, hips and hind legs.

7 CHAKRAS

Yoga is an eastern discipline that recognizes the existence of energy pathways and centers. Many eastern traditions believe that energy runs through and around the physical body.

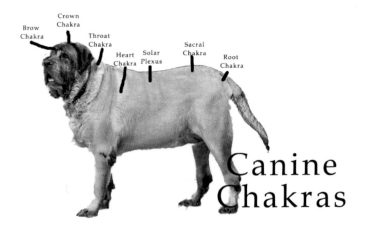

This energy is known by many different names. In the Far East it is called *Chi*. In Yoga it is called *Prana*. It is believed to be the life force that flows through tissue, organs, and systems. When a blockage or imbalance exists, yoga practitioners believe that health suffers.

These energy centers are the rationale behind acupuncture, and the seven major centers are called *chakras*. Each chakra is associated with certain physical and emotional qualities. Apparently animals and humans have these centers.

To balance your dog's chakras, gently tap your dog on the chakra points, just as you would do for yourself.

Root Chakra—the sacrum: This chakra is located at the base of spine in humans and the base of the tail in dogs.

The root chakra corresponds with the lower spine, hips, legs and feet. It is associated with elimination and the colon. In dogs it also affects the adrenals and kidneys. Emotionally it is associated with survival--food, shelter, and security. When this area is stable, you and your dog feel assured that your needs will be met. The element associated with this chakra is earth. The color is red.

Second Chakra—the pelvis. This chakra, referred to as the sacral in dogs only, is located in the lower abdomen in humans and in the abdominal cavity of dogs. In humans this chakra affects the reproductive organs, the bladder, the pelvis and hips, the intestines, the kidneys and adrenals. In dogs it affects the pelvis, bladder, reproductive organs, large and small intestines, and the stomach. Emotionally this chakra is associated with creativity and being able to "go with the flow." The element is water and the color is orange.

Third Chakra—the solar plexus. In humans this energy center is located in the mid to upper abdomen. In dogs it is located in the upper chest, a few inches behind the front legs. It is associated with the digestive organs. This chakra influences the stomach, gallbladder, pancreas, liver, diaphragm, kidneys, and nervous system. Emotionally this center has to do with assimilating energy and power.

Here you digest food and emotions. Good health is dependent on proper assimilation of nutrients and good mental health is dependent on the proper processing of emotions. Your sense of will power, drive, and force reside here. Anger also resides in the third chakra. The element is fire. The color is yellow.

Fourth Chakra—the heart. In humans and dogs this energy center is located at the heart. It affects the circulatory, respiratory, and immune systems. Emotionally it is associated with love—the love is extended to ourselves as well as others.

Our dogs teach us a great deal about unconditional love. Canine family members live to love us. They always forgive and would lay down their lives to protect us. Our dogs help us expand our ability to love. The element associated with this chakra is air and the color is green.

Fifth Chakra--the throat. In humans and dogs this chakra is located in the throat and includes the neck, esophagus, voice mechanism, mouth and teeth, and thyroid. In dogs this energy center influences the thyroid, lungs, respiratory system, forelegs, paws, mouth, throat, and the vocal system. In both species it relates to the ability to communicate. The element associated with this chakra is the ether, or sky. The color associated with this chakra is blue.

Sixth Chakra—the brow. This chakra is located in the forehead, slightly above the eyes, in both humans and dogs. In humans it is associated with intuition, insight, clarity and the pituitary gland. In dogs it is associated with the nervous system and concentration. The element associated with this chakra is light, and the corresponding color is violet.

Seventh Chakra--the crown: In humans this chakra is located at the top of the head at the fontanel. In dogs it is located at the top of the head between the ears. In humans it is associated with our pineal glands and relates to our ability to connect to the universal energy and embodies our sense of connection. In dogs it is associated with the cranium. The element associated with this chakra is space or thought, and the color of the seventh chakra is crystal.

This information is provided for your information. If your dog is in pain, you might try tapping the appropriate chakra point to see if that will bring some relief. Acupuncturists use this science to bring pain relief, so you may be able to find similar success at home.

8 BREATHING

Breathing practices, called *pranayam*, are essential to yoga. Linking the breath to our physical practice is what sets yoga apart from other exercise. Your breath is a direct road to your nervous system. Breathing practices help us relax, center, focus, deal with pain, sleep better, and rise to higher levels of consciousness.

Many other disciplines have used breathing practices for these purposes. Natural childbirth modifies the breath to help deal with pain. Psychology uses breathing techniques for stress management, anxiety and depression. Many athletic disciplines use breathing techniques to enhance performance. Most of these techniques have their roots in yogic practice.

Here are some basic techniques of pranayam, the breath practice. *Prana* means the life force and *yam* is the study of that force. It is believed that the life force enters with the breath and is distributed and altered though breath management. Doga allows you to do these techniques with your dog.

The following practices can be done seated with your dog in your lap or at your side. You can even lie down with your chest and head elevated with your dog on your chest or belly.

Satisfying Breath: The first practice to master is simply breath awareness and finding your satisfying breath. Begin breathing naturally and notice how you breathe. Notice the depth and rhythm of your natural breath. Don't change it, just observe. Then try the make it the most satisfying breath that brings you enough oxygen. Find a breath that is comfortable and satisfying. This would be your baseline for further practice. You would then work on making it longer and deeper while keeping it calm and satisfying.

Belly Breath: Relax your belly completely and inhale to the belly, filling it with air. When you do this your diaphragm will move down, making room in your lungs for oxygen. As you exhale, pull your belly in and push the breath out. The inhale and exhale originate from the navel center, about three fingers' width below your belly button. This is a very relaxing and easy breath to learn. Your dog can rest on your belly or by your side if you are reclined. If you are seated, your dog can sit in your lap.

Chest Breath: low lung, mid lung, upper lung. This is a breath where you fill the lower lungs first and then the mid and upper lungs. This breath takes some practice. You inhale to your lower lungs and let the lower ribs expand. Then fill to the mid lungs and let the mid ribs expand, then all the way up to the collarbone. Then exhale from the top down. Again, you can do this in a reclined or seated position with your dog cuddling on your lap or belly.

Long Deep Breathing. This technique combines the first two. You begin with an abdominal breath, filling your belly. Then, fill your lungs from the bottom to the top. Then exhale from the top off the lungs down, releasing the belly last.

Segmented Breath: In this breath we pause as we inhale and exhale. You suspend the breath without tightness. You could start by breaking the inhale into two parts. Inhale to half capacity . . . suspend the breath . . . inhale to full capacity. Then exhale completely. You could then try suspending the breath on the exhale. Halt at halfway exhaled and then exhale fully. You could even suspend at the beginning of the inhale and end of the exhale.

Once your have mastered a two-phase inhale, try attempting four phases on the inhale and four on the exhale. Remember to keep the exercise calm and satisfying. You should not experience anxiety while doing breath work.

Alternate Nostril Breath: This breath works on breathing through with one nostril at a time. In yogic teachings it is believed that breathing through the left nostril promotes a sense of calm while breathing through the right nostril is energizing and brings alertness. Medical studies have shown that we breathe through different nostrils throughout the day, and one side is usually more open than the other. You notice this most when you have a cold. But which nostril your breathe through does have an effect on your body.

Alternating between left and right nostrils keeps your hormones balanced. It also balances both hemispheres of the brain. When the right nostril is open you access the left hemisphere and when the right nostril is open you access the left hemisphere. The yogis have known this for ages and have manipulated the mind and mood by breathing though only one nostril or both in a controlled way.

Begin by closing off the right nostril and breathe deeply through your left nostril only. This is calming and accesses the right brain. This can also help you get to sleep at night. Then close off the left nostril and breathe only through the right nostril. This is energizing and accesses the left-brain. Notice the effect of breathing through only one nostril. If the nostril is blocked you can pull on the skin by the side of your nose to open the nostril.

Once you have breathed through each nostril independently, begin to put them together. Inhale through our left nostril and exhale through your right. Do this for a while and notice the effects. Than inhale through your right nostril and exhale through your left. Notice the effects.

Try inhaling right and exhaling left, and keep alternating in this way. This is a balancing breath practice that soothes and clams while maintaining alertness and awareness. This breathing exercise is best done seated with your dog in your lap or by your side.

Breath of Fire: This is a powerful breath with many benefits. It increases oxygen in the blood, uplifts mood and can balance energy in the body. It is a faster breath that moves from the navel center. The navel expands with the inhale and recedes with the exhale. It is a bit like panting or sniffing.

You inhale and exhale through the nose. It is best to do this breath seated.

P.S. Take lessons from your dog.

9 MEDITATIONS

I'm happy to offer several meditations you can do with your dog. These are traditional meditation techniques that have been adapted to incorporate your best canine pal.

Heart Beat per Your Breath: One meditation in yoga involves finding your pulse and focusing on your heartbeat. It's done with a relaxed breath. Your mental focus should be on the steady beat of your heart. Sometimes we add a mental mantra to synchronize with the rhythm of our pulse.

This technique can also be done with our dogs. We start by tuning in to our own heartbeat and staying focused. Then we find our dog's heartbeat and focus on that. Compare your dog's rhythm to yours. This is a wonderful practice to develop focus and attention skills.

Breath per Breath: The following meditation is similar to the heart beat meditation. You begin by tuning in to your own breath and then tune in to your dog's. Compare the two and keep focused.

Awareness: This is a variation of mindfulness meditation where you focus on your dog. Experience your dog with all your senses. Stoke her fur and feel every sensation. Look at your dog and focus on details, the color of her eyes, fur, feet, texture, etc. Then breathe in the scent of your dog, really parsing the fragrance as though you were trying to memorize it.

Healing Visualization: This technique utilizes visualization. Place your hand on your dog and send healing energy to the area of concern. Then visualize the area working properly. Visualize your dog being healthy and happy.

Savasana

We end each doga class with a ten-minute relaxation period called *savasana.*

When we lie down our dog's first instinct is to protect us. This comes from the covered wagon camping days when dogs stayed up all night guarding the camp and their people.

When we first lie down with our dogs, we have to lie in a comfortable position similar to how we'd normally cuddle. This is different than the traditional position for savasana where we lie flat on our backs with palms up and feet mat-width apart. Get into a comfortable flat position so your dog will feel secure. Cuddle and stroke your pet. Let your breathing slow.

When we relax, our muscles soften and we feel a sense of release. Our bodies begin to sink. Our joints release. Our breathing and heart rate slow.

Once you have settled, begin to systematically relax your body. Begin with your toes--big toes, second toes, third toes, fourth toes, and pinkie toes. You can do one foot at a time or start at the tips of your toes and move toward your head. Next relax your feet, legs, hips and buttocks, lower back, mid back, upper back and shoulder blades, ribs, shoulders, arms, hands, fingers, neck and throat, inside of the mouth, tongue, jaw, outside of the face, lips, cheeks, brows, eyebrows, eyelids. Let the back of your head sink to the floor. Let your whole body feel as if it's so liquid it could sink into the floor.

When your dog feels you relax, he will relax, too. One of the things that amazes us most in doga classes is that at this point, even with twenty dogs and their owners in the room, every living creature is drifting in deep relaxation.

All in all, a beautiful experience.

ABOUT THE AUTHOR

Lisa Recchione, MA, E-RYT, KRI Certified

A student of many yoga styles, Lisa is certified in Hatha Yoga and Kundalini Yoga. She has studied various techniques including alignment-based yoga, therapeutic yoga, Kundalini yoga, and Vinyasa yoga. She has also studied many styles of meditation and breath practice.

Prior to teaching yoga and meditation, Lisa worked in the fields of Special Education, Counseling, and Social Work. She has a Masters Degree in Counseling.

She teaches a variety of styles in varied settings and works with special populations in assisted living and nursing facilities. She has worked with people facing many different challenges including Parkinson's, Alzheimer's, MS, stroke, Huntington's, arthritis, back injury and more. She also teaches Hatha and Kundalini classes, and of course Doga.

Married for twenty-five years, she and her husband have two grown children. Her two furry children are Ollie and Maggie, the Morkie and Maltese featured in many of the photos.

Lisa first adopted Ollie when her father, whom Lisa cared for in her home, was diagnosed with Alzheimer's. She had read about the benefits of dog therapy for people with dementia and thought it might be beneficial to have a dog.

Ollie was an angel of light bringing joy not only to Lisa's father, but also to the whole family. The healing love of that little entity was boundless. After Lisa's father passed away, the family adopted Maggie and were doubly blessed. Dogs, Lisa believes, are the embodiment of infinite, unconditional love. For this reason, she has begun to share that love with others in her yoga classes.

"People instantly relax when they have a dog in their lap," she says. "I teach them how to stroke the dogs and the dogs relax. I have seen smiles on faces that rarely smile. I even heard a woman with Alzheimer's tell me her dog that looked like mine. The nurse's aid said that the woman rarely spoke. Holding the dog helped her access deep feelings and memories of her dog from years ago. Some residents call them little babies and rock them.

"One group has adopted my dogs as their grand-dogs. It is truly heart expanding. I begin these classes by letting the dogs acclimate while we stretch and do our exercises. The people can call the dogs and pick them up anytime during the class. Before the relaxation period I take the dogs around and give each person a chance to hold and stroke and cuddle these furry little animals. My dogs love this as much as the residents.

"There are many opportunities for a willing dog owner to incorporate his or her dog into therapy work. The dog, however, needs to be friendly, potty trained, not aggressive, leash trained, and not prone to barking.

"I hope that the practice of doga will help you appreciate your canine companion even more. And as you grow close to your pet, I hope you will consider sharing that love with others who could use a hug or a canine kiss."

We hope you have enjoyed this book, and we'd be honored if you would leave a book review on Amazon.com. Thank you for your support. If you have any questions or comments, please write us at lisarecchioneyoga@gmail.com.

Lisa Recchione, MA, E-RYT, KRI Certified

www.LearnYogawithLisa.com
February 2014

LISA RECCHIONE YOGA
Wellness, Growth, Joy

Notes:

Printed in Poland
by Amazon Fulfillment
Poland Sp. z o.o., Wrocław

51385612R00047